MW01148081

Saints for Girls

NIHIL OBSTAT: John A, Goodwine, J.C.D.
                  Censor Librorum

IMPRIMATUR: ✛ Francis Cardinal Spellman
                  Archbishop of New York
                  April 11, 1961

Published by Neumann Press, an imprint of TAN Books. Originally published as: *Saints for Girls* and *More Saints for Girls,* Guild Press, 1961; *Saint Bernadette* and *Saint Therese*, Guild Press, 1957. Revised edition with color corrections, cover design copyright © Neumann Press.

ISBN: 978-1-939094-19-3

Printed and bound in the United States of America.

Neumann Press
Charlotte, North Carolina
www.NeumannPress.com
2014

SAINTS FOR GIRLS

by SUSAN WEAVER

pictures by CATHERINE BARNES

Nihil obstat: John A. Goodwine, J.C.D., Censor Librorum
Imprimatur: ✠ Francis Cardinal Spellman, Archbishop of New York
April 11, 1961

NEUMANN PRESS

Contents

SAINT GENEVIEVE

Long ago, a young girl named Genevieve lived in Paris. One day enemy soldiers came and camped outside the city. They would not let anyone go into the city and they would not let anyone leave it.

Before long, the people had eaten every bit of food they had, and they were very hungry.

The soldiers shouted, "You will all starve if you do not give your city to us."

Genevieve prayed hard, and she wondered what she could do to help her people. One day she walked to the river that ran through the city. Suddenly she had an idea.

That night Genevieve and some of her friends crept to the river and got onto rafts. In the darkness, they sailed quietly down the river and past the soldiers.

At a country place Genevieve and her friends piled food on the rafts. Then, before morning, they sailed back to the city.

How happy the hungry people were to see the food. Everyone cheered, and they thanked Genevieve for saving their city.

Years later, another enemy was ready to attack Paris. Again Genevieve begged God to save her people. She prayed so hard that God kept the enemy from coming to Paris. Once more the city was saved.

Genevieve was a brave young woman, and today the people of Paris pray to her to watch over them.

Genevieve can help you, too, and be your friend. If ever you are a little bit afraid, think of Saint Genevieve and her brave trust in God.

SAINT ELIZABETH

Once upon a time there was a little princess named Elizabeth. She lived in a palace, and she could have anything she wanted.

But Elizabeth did not keep her toys just for herself. She would call to other boys and girls, "Come and share my things."

Elizabeth grew up and married a prince named Louis. He was good, like Elizabeth, and they were very happy. After a few years, Louis and Elizabeth became king and queen.

Once Louis had to go on a long trip, and Elizabeth ruled the country for him. Times were very hard and many poor people were hungry. But Elizabeth gave food to everyone who needed it.

Many people were sick, too, and Elizabeth sold her jewels and built hospitals. Then she worked in the hospitals as a nurse.

When King Louis came home, his mother said, "Elizabeth is giving all your money to the poor. Soon you will be poor yourself."

King Louis said, "Mother, you must not say anything against Elizabeth. She is good, and everything she does is good, too."

Queen Elizabeth did not want to make her husband's mother unhappy. And so, when she carried bread to the poor, she hid it under her robe.

One day Elizabeth met a man who knew the king's mother. He said, "Queen Elizabeth, may I see what you are carrying?"

The queen was carrying bread. She knew that if the man saw it, he would tell the king's mother. With a prayer she opened the robe.

There was no bread in her arms! It had all turned to red roses.

Elizabeth thanked God for helping her, and she went on being kind to the poor.

All this happened long ago, but even today hospitals are named for Saint Elizabeth, and doctors and nurses pray to her, too. We can try to be like her by being kind to others.

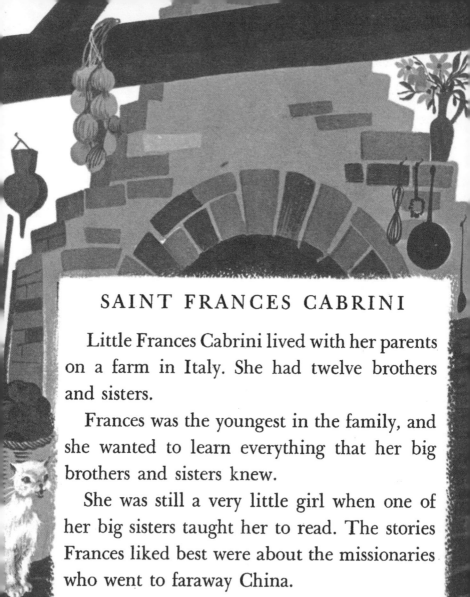

SAINT FRANCES CABRINI

Little Frances Cabrini lived with her parents on a farm in Italy. She had twelve brothers and sisters.

Frances was the youngest in the family, and she wanted to learn everything that her big brothers and sisters knew.

She was still a very little girl when one of her big sisters taught her to read. The stories Frances liked best were about the missionaries who went to faraway China.

Frances thought and thought about the brave missionaries who left their homes to go to China. Soon she wanted more than anything else to be a missionary, too.

One summer day, she and her big sister took picnic lunches and sat near a little brook. After lunch, Frances made paper boats and filled them with wild flowers.

She said to her sister, "All the flowers are missionaries. They are going to sail down the brook, out to the ocean, and all the way to China in the paper boats."

Her sister laughed and said, "Oh, Frances, I am afraid your boats will sink before they go very far."

"No, no!" said Frances. "God will take care of them."

Frances grew up and became a sister, but she still wanted to be a missionary. Then, one day, the Pope sent for her. He said, "Sister, I want you to go to America to help the people."

Frances did not like ships and the sea, but she thought, "God will take care of me." Then she went aboard a big ship and sailed across the sea to America with other sisters.

She traveled all over the country, building schools for children and hospitals for the sick. She worked hard and everyone loved her.

Frances traveled to many countries, but she became a citizen of the United States. After Frances died, she was the first citizen of this country to be made a saint.

Saint Frances Cabrini always said, "Love one another. Be kind, and never be sharp or harsh." Don't you think these are good words to remember?

More
Saints for Girls

by EVE ROUKE
pictures by
MIRCEA VASILIU

Saint Helena

SAINT HELENA was born in Britain a long time ago. When she grew up she married a Roman general. Their son, Constantine, became a very important man, the ruler of the Roman Empire.

One day Constantine told Helena that he wanted to build a church in the Holy Land. He asked her to go there to take charge of this work.

When she arrived in Jerusalem, she said to the Bishop, Saint Macarius, "Show me where our Lord died. We will build our church there."

"A pagan temple has been built over the place where He died," said the Bishop.

"Let us tear it down," said Helena. Then she asked him, "Do you know what happened to the Cross on which our Lord was crucified?"

"No one knows," answered the Bishop. "It has never been found."

"Maybe we will find It when we tear down the temple," said Helena.

Some say Helena then dreamed where the Cross was. When workmen dug at that spot, they found three crosses.

No one could tell which Cross was our Lord's. But when a dying woman was touched with the third Cross, she was instantly cured.

A beautiful church was built where the Cross was found and Helena often went there to pray. She used her great wealth to build many other churches and to help the poor.

We remember Saint Helena today not only because she found the True Cross, but because, although she was an Empress, she was still God's humble servant.

Saint Brigid

Saint Brigid was born a very long time ago in Ireland. Her father was a chieftain, but her mother was a slave. So Brigid was a slave, too. Her mother was sent to a family far away and Brigid always wanted to go to visit her.

At last, Brigid was given her freedom and the first thing she did was to go to her mother. She was ill and unable to work. Brigid then milked all the cows and made the butter so her mother could rest.

Brigid was kind and good to everyone. Soon many beggars discovered that she would never say "No" to them.

The master heard about Brigid's kindness to the poor. He said to his wife, "Let us go to the dairy and make sure that Brigid does not give away too much of our food."

They took a big basket and went to find Brigid. They told her they had come for the butter.

While Brigid put butter into the basket, she asked God to let there be enough for the master. When she gave the basket to him, it was full.

The master knew then that God was with Brigid. He told her he would give her all the cows in his herd.

But Brigid said to him, "I do not want your cows."

"What then?" asked the master.

"I want my mother to be free," answered Brigid. And the master allowed it.

35

Now that her mother was free, Brigid could become a nun as she had always wanted. She founded many convents with the help of the bishops of Ireland.

Of all the women who have ever lived in Ireland, Saint Brigid is the most loved. In that country not only girls are named in her honor, but rivers and brooks, flowers as well as churches.

Saint Brigid was never known to be unhappy no matter what happened to her. From her we can learn that being happy and holy belong together very naturally.

Saint Teresa

Saint Teresa lived in Spain in very exciting times. The Moors had conquered much of that country, and many Christians had been killed fighting against them.

One day Teresa was playing with one of her brothers. She said to him, "I wish we could fight the Moors, too."

"We might be killed," Rodrigo said.

"All the better," said Teresa. "If we die fighting for our Lord we will be martyrs. Martyrs, you know, go straight to Heaven. Let's go and fight the Moors."

The next morning Teresa and Rodrigo tiptoed out of the house before anyone was awake. They walked along, talking about God and how they would fight the Moors for Him.

The children were quite a distance from home when they saw a man on horseback. When he came closer they saw he was their uncle.

"What are you doing here?" he asked them in surprise.

"We are going to fight the Moors," said Teresa.

"Oh no," said their uncle. "You are going home to your mother. When you are older you can find a way of giving your life to God."

And indeed, God had great plans for Teresa. When she grew up, she became a Carmelite nun.

Convents at that time were not at all like those of today. Many of the nuns wanted to serve God better, but there were no other convents to go to. So Teresa started a new kind of convent where the nuns lived very strict lives.

Once Teresa was trying to found a new convent and had very little money. But she said, "Teresa and a few cents are nothing. God and Teresa and a few cents are enough."

Saint Teresa had great trust in our Lord. Perhaps we can learn to trust Him as she did.

Teresa was often tired and ill and even hungry, but she founded many convents. And she wrote books about God for her nuns that even now we read because they are among the most wonderful books ever written.

Saint Bernadette

BY FATHER GALES
Pictures by CATHERINE BARNES

Nihil obstat: JOHN A GOODWINE, J.C.D., Censor Librorum
Imprimatur: ✠ FRANCIS CARDINAL SPELLMAN, Archbishop of New York
May 15, 1957

Saint Bernadette was born in the little town of Lourdes. It is in France, a country far away.

Bernadette's father worked in flour mills, but he could not keep a job.

That is why her mother had to work to get food and clothing for the family.

Little Bernadette had to take care
of the smaller children. And she had to clean
the house. She had no time for play.
She could not even go to school
until she was fourteen years old.

But Bernadette was always cheerful
because she offered Jesus everything she did.

Bernadette's mother taught her to pray.
The little girl began her work every day
with the *Our Father.*

When she came to the words,
"Thy will be done on earth as it is in heaven,"
she smiled. The smile stayed on her face
while she scrubbed the floor or did the washing.

Bernadette was not healthy.
The work was really too hard for her.
But when she was weak,
she thought how Jesus had suffered.
She remembered the prayer of Jesus,
"Not My will but Thine be done."
Then she felt strong again
to go on with her work.

Every day Bernadette prayed also
to our Lady, the Blessed Mother of Jesus.
And the Blessed Virgin had a special love
for this little girl.

Bernadette's greatest wish was
to go to school and learn how to receive Jesus
in Holy Communion.

In the summertime, Bernadette had to watch
the sheep. Every day she would kneel
at our Lady's shrine and pray
that her wish would come true.

And our Lady heard the girl's prayer.
When Bernadette was fourteen,
the Sisters of Charity took her
into their school to learn to read and write.
Soon she could make her first Holy Communion.
How happy Bernadette was!

About a month after her fourteenth birthday, on February 11, 1858, the most wonderful thing happened to Bernadette.

She and two other girls of poor families went down to the river to pick up driftwood and fallen branches. Bernadette was not as quick as the other girls.
She stayed behind.

Suddenly she heard a sound in the bare rocks.
It was like wind in the woods.

Bernadette looked upward. There she saw
a beautiful Lady standing in a niche in the rocks.

A golden light
was around the Lady.
And roses bloomed
at her feet.

The girl was afraid,
but the Lady smiled
and waved her
to come nearer.

Bernadette fell
on her knees
in wonder and prayer.

Then the two girls came back to look
for Bernadette. She was still kneeling,
holding her rosary in her folded hands.

Bernadette told the two girls
what she had seen. They laughed mockingly
and wanted to know what the Lady had said.

"She said nothing," answered Bernadette.
"She only held a rosary in her hands
and she prayed the *Gloria* with me
after each decade. And at the end of the Rosary
she disappeared."

The girls began to bind up their twigs.
All the time they kept on teasing Bernadette.

Bernadette did not know
that it was the Blessed Virgin
whom she had seen. Nobody believed her
when she told about the Lady—
not even the sisters and her pastor,
Father Peyramale.

But Bernadette kept going to the river.
She saw the Lady many more times.

Once our Lady asked the girl
to pray for sinners.

Another time, to show that she was from God,
she told Bernadette to dig in the dry ground.
When the girl did so, healing water bubbled up.

The water still cures people today.

On March 25, 1858, Bernadette said
to the Lady:
"Father Peyramale wants to know who you are."
The Lady answered:
"I am the Immaculate Conception."
This means the Mother of Jesus
was free from Adam's sin.
And then the Lady said:
"I want a church built here."

The people began to believe
that it was really the Blessed Virgin
who came to see Bernadette.

Bernadette's work seemed to be finished now.
She entered a convent.

When the first Mass was said
in the church of Our Lady of Lourdes,
important people from everywhere were there.
But Bernadette was not there.
She was in the convent, praying for sinners.

Many people wanted
to meet Bernadette.
But she did not want people
to make a fuss over her.
One day,
as she swept the hall,
a man came up to her
and said:
"Please, tell me
how I can see Bernadette."
Bernadette answered
with a smile:
"Keep your eye
on that doorway
and you will see her
slip through."

And that was just
what she did
a little while later.

Bernadette died in the year 1879.
She had been sick for seven long years.
Pope Pius named her a saint
on December 8, 1933.
Every year on this day
we celebrate the Feast
of the Immaculate Conception.

Saint Agnes

SAINT AGNES learned all about God when she was a child. Her mother said, "People who hate Jesus will try to get you to do bad things. You must love God so much that you will always say NO to anything bad."

When Agnes was thirteen a rich man asked her to marry him. Agnes said "NO!" It would be wrong for her to marry anyone, because she had promised her love to Jesus. The man was so angry he had Agnes killed. She was a martyr —which means she died for Jesus.

Dear Saint Agnes, help me to suffer
rather than do anything bad.

Saint Margaret Mary

SAINT MARGARET MARY received Jesus in Holy Communion when she was very young. You also receive Jesus when you go to Holy Communion.

Margaret Mary became a Sister. One day Jesus said to her, "Tell everybody how much I love them. I want them to love Me more and more."

Jesus promised many blessings to those who love His Sacred Heart and receive Him in Holy Communion.

You gave me Your Heart, dear Jesus—I give You mine.

SAINT THERESE

BY FATHER GALES
Pictures by WILLIAM DE J. RUTHERFOORD

Nihil obstat: JOHN A. GOODWINE, J.C.D., Censor Librorum
Imprimatur: ✠ FRANCIS CARDINAL SPELLMAN, Archbishop of New York
May 15, 1957

One evening, when Saint Therese was
five years old, she was out walking
with her father.

Therese looked up to the stars.

All at once she cried: "Look, Papa!
My name is written in the sky!"

Her father smiled and said: "You are right,
those stars do make a T."

From that evening on, Therese wanted
to learn all she could about heaven.
She asked her sister Pauline to help her.
Pauline took care of Therese,
for their mother was dead.

Therese was the baby of the family,
and she was a little spoiled.

But now she begged Pauline
to help her to get over
being stubborn.

Pauline wanted to show her little sister
why some souls are happier in heaven than others.
She filled a cup and a thimble to the brim.
Then she said to Therese: "Look here!
The cup is full and the thimble is full.

"But the cup holds much more. So it is
with the happiness of souls in heaven.

"If you make more room in your soul for God,
your happiness in heaven will be greater."

This was a lesson easy to learn!

Therese began to give up little things
for the love of God. By the time she was nine,
Therese had become very gentle and good.

Now Pauline felt that her own wish
could come true, and so she entered a convent.

In the year that followed, Therese was
suffering from a sickness. No doctor was able
to help her.

But God sent our Lady to cure the little girl.

While she was sick, Therese learned
a big secret. She wrote it down for us:

"We show our love for God when we are
patient in suffering. By this suffering
we make good for the sins of others."

Therese heard about a prisoner
who refused to be sorry for his crime.

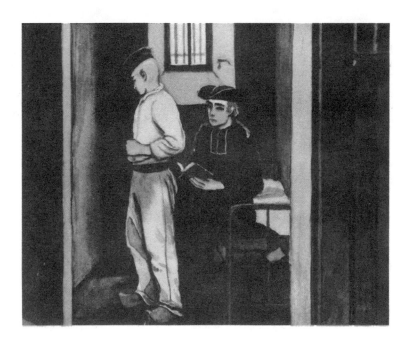

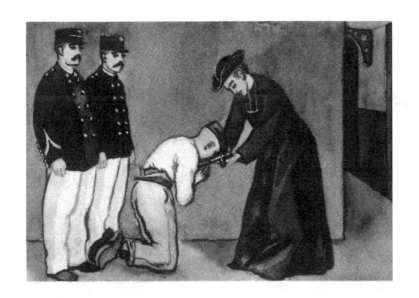

Therese did penance and prayed.
She asked God for a sign that the soul
of the sinner would be saved.

Then Therese learned that the man
had asked for a crucifix and kissed it
three times at the very last moment
of his life.

Therese was very happy to learn
that her prayers were answered.

One Christmas Eve, a few days before
her fourteenth birthday, God gave Therese
the most wonderful gift anyone ever got.

The girl's room was all at once filled
with heavenly light. In the midst of it
she saw the sweet face of the Child Jesus.

Soon after, Therese told her father
that God wanted her to become a Carmelite nun.
Everyone said she was too young. But her father
took her to Rome to see the pope.

Therese was told not to speak to the pope.
But she did not think it wrong to talk
to His Holiness the Pope about something
that is for God's glory.

So Therese said: "Holy Father! I have
a great favor to ask. Will you allow me
to enter the convent when I am fifteen?
Holy Father, please say yes!"

Pope Leo XIII was taken by surprise.
He said: "You shall enter Carmel if it is
God's will." — And it was God's will!

The following year, Therese entered
the convent to live entirely for God.

She remembered her wonderful Christmas gift
from God and took the name of Sister Therese
of the Child Jesus.

Therese wanted to be a martyr
like Saint Agnes was. If Therese could not give
her blood, she would give all her love.
She would bear with patience all suffering
for the love of Jesus.

Therese kept her promise. For several years
she suffered the greatest pains.

Therese lived only nine years in the convent.

In these years she wrote the story of her life.

Saint Therese wants everyone to know about her "Little Ways" of following God.

Here are some of her sayings:

"It is so consoling to call God *our Father!*"

"We are too small
to do great things for God.
So we should do
many little things for Him
with a great love."

"We must be childlike
before we can become
Christlike."

"After my death I will
send a shower of roses."

Her last words were:
"My God...I...love...You!"

Therese died in 1897 at the age of twenty-four. The Church named her a saint in 1925. Two years later, Pope Pius XI named her a special guardian saint of the foreign missions — because Saint Therese offered her life for the work of priests and missioners.

Before We Begin to Pray

REMEMBER that God is close to us, looking at us and listening to us. Remember that He loves us, and wants us to talk to Him.

Morning Prayer to the Guardian Angel

Angel of God, my guardian dear,
To whom His love commits me here;
Ever this day be at my side,
To light and guard, to rule and guide.
Amen.

WHEN we are born, God gives each one of us a brave, bright angel to watch over us and take care of us. The angel is our guardian. He stays with us while we grow. All through life, the angel is at our side. When we die, the angel takes our soul to God.

The Sign of the Cross

*In the Name of the Father, and of the Son,
and of the Holy Ghost, Amen.*

In the Name of the Father

and of the Son *and of the Holy Ghost* *Amen.*

THE SIGN of the cross is the most beautiful of all signs. It means that there is One God, who is great and good and beautiful, and that He is Three Persons. The First Person is God the Father, who made us out of nothing. The Second Person is God the Son, who came from heaven to save us. His name is Jesus. He comes to live in us in Holy Communion. The Third Person is God the Holy Ghost. He is all love and goodness. He makes things live and grow, and He helps us to be holy.

The sign of the cross reminds us that Jesus, the Son of God, died on a cross. He died in such a hard way because He loves us and wants us to love Him.

We should make the sign of the cross carefully and with love. Then good and holy thoughts fill our hearts.

We make the sign of the cross when we wake up, and before we go to sleep. We make it when we go into church, and before and after we pray, and before we eat or drink. We often make it before we go somewhere, or when we begin to work or play. Then we do these things in God's Name, to please Him, and God blesses us.

The Our Father

Our Father, who art in Heaven, hallowed be Thy Name. Thy Kingdom come, Thy Will be done on earth, as it is in heaven. Give us this day our daily bread, and forgive us our trespasses, as we forgive those who trespass against us. And lead us not into temptation, but deliver us from evil. Amen.

WHEN JESUS, God's Son, came down from heaven to be with us, He had many things to teach us. He wanted to tell us about God, His Father. He wanted to tell us about what heaven is like, and what we should do to go there. The people had seen Him pray to God, His Father, every day, and sometimes all night. One day someone asked Him, "Lord, teach us how to pray." And so Jesus taught them the Our Father.

The Our Father is the best of all prayers. When we say it, Jesus prays with us. That makes our prayers very strong and holy, because Jesus is God. We pray with Jesus, and with all the Christian people in the world. Our prayers go up to God all together, like one big voice.

The Our Father teaches us that we should not spend all our time asking God for things. We should start out by loving and praising God, and we should pray for God's Kingdom—for God to be known and loved everywhere. We should forgive other people who have been mean to us, if we want God to forgive us our sins. And we should ask God to help us be good.

The Hail Mary

Hail Mary, full of grace! The Lord is with thee; blessed art thou among women, and blessed is the fruit of thy womb, Jesus. Holy Mary, Mother of God, pray for us sinners, now and at the hour of our death. Amen.

WE CANNOT look straight at the sun. It is too bright and beautiful. God is bright and beautiful too, and we cannot see Him with our eyes. His brightness is called "grace."

When God made the first man and woman, Adam and Eve, their souls were bright with grace. But Adam and Eve did not stay good. They sinned and lost God's grace. After that, nobody in the world had any grace. Nobody was fit to be God's friend. Heaven's door was shut. A dead bird or a dead kitten is not like a live one. Life is gone. Grace is God's life. People's souls are dead when they have no grace.

God wanted to give us grace again. He started by making a new little girl with grace in her soul. The little girl's name was Mary. When Mary grew up to be a young lady, God sent one of His great angels to visit her.

The angel bowed low, and said, "Hail, Mary, full of grace! The Lord is with thee!"

The angel told Mary a secret. He told her she was going to have a baby, and the baby would be God's Son!

Mary said, "I will do whatever God wants."

After a while Mary's baby was born. His name was Jesus. Jesus is God's Son, and He has God's brightness and beauty. That is what we mean when we say, "Blessed is the fruit of thy womb, Jesus." That is what Mary's cousin, Elizabeth, said when Mary came to visit her.

When Jesus grew up, He died on the cross and opened heaven for us. He brought back grace for everybody in the whole world. Mary stood by the cross and cried when Jesus died. We want Mary to pray for us now and when we die, too. We say, "Holy Mary, Mother of God, pray for us sinners, now and at the hour of our death. Amen."

NEUMANN PRESS | *A collection of the finest*
Catholic children's books

978-1-930873-35-3

978-0-911845-19-8

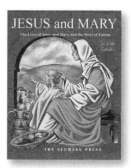

978-1-930873-42-1

978-0-911845-66-2

978-0-911845-67-9

978-0-911845-94-5

978-0-911845-95-2

www.NeumannPress.com • (800) 437-5876

978-0-911845-03-7

978-0-911845-04-4

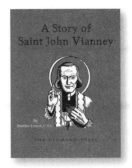

978-0-911845-30-3

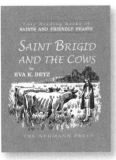

978-1-930873-95-7

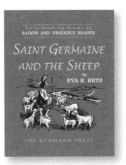

978-1-930873-96-4

978-1-930873-83-4

978-0-911845-46-4

978-0-911845-47-1

978-0-911845-48-8

978-0-911845-49-5

www.NeumannPress.com • (800) 437-5876

NEUMANN PRESS

Neumann Press, an imprint of TAN Books, publishes books and materials for children that educate, inspire, and assist their first steps in the Catholic faith.

Neumann Press was established in 1981 by the Dennis McCoy family. The Press became known and loved by thousands of customers for its nearly 200 classic Catholic titles, each one lovingly and expertly printed and bound by McCoy family members and friends.

In 2013 Neumann Press was acquired by TAN. Today Neumann Press continues to publish the vintage children and educational titles for which it is loved—as well as releasing new titles that raise the hearts and minds of children to God.

For a free catalog, visit us online at
NeumannPress.com

Or call us toll-free at
(800) 437-5876